Advance praise for *Last Horizon*

It's never too late to begin in earnest to try to come to terms with life and living by expressing yourself through the Arts, and John Hickman, urged on by his "muse and mentor," Laura Hope Gill, uses poetry to do just that. In Last Horizon, while asserting the truism that "Dying is easy. Living—that's what's hard," he has found that "Poetry does heal." Being "Too old for youth / Too young to die", In celebrating the voices of a residential writing group - "I reveled in their cheer amid the pains of aging. / They leave stories. / Stories are eternal!" - he praises one of the gifts (and difficulties) of writing, the saying of oneself. Towards the end of Last Horizon we read, "The snowflakes continue to fall. / Not enough for white. / But enough." This life-lived, clear-eyed coupling of disappointment-meets-hope-and-acceptance is typical of John Hickman the man, and of his story, and bodes well for his attempts in healing verse to push back against that last horizon.

—**Adrian Rice,** *The Strange Estate*

These poems are a type of taking account of what it is to be human, especially as that human looks towards the inevitable. Perhaps that is the Last Horizon, the one we cannot know until we get there. The one that is more about what came before but comes also to end.

—**Steven Jones, Asheville**

Who is immune to poetry that says, "Let's be friends, I and me?" John Hickman's poems are lyrical in Holy Ground: "Hush—my children, can't you see," tender in Sudden Death: "Dying is easy. Living—that's what's hard," and spiritually responsible in "Anthropos": "It was on that day that you learned to subdue your earth…You subdued it all right!/Noxious compounds increased your harvests." Hickman's poetry makes you laugh, breathe, think, and sigh as he takes you through the processes and horizons of life. This collection will titillate your mind and heart, and make you want more.

—**Madelyn Edwards,** *The Catfish Trilogy*

In this beautiful work, John Hickman addresses the essential human experiences of intimacy, place, and spirit. He shares his broad and deep understanding of the world and his place in it to express in poetic words wisdom that goes beyond words.

—**Sally Atkins,**
Nature-Based Expressive Arts Therapy

John Hickman is an imaginative and enterprising sailor on the ocean of life. His poetry choices will carry you through your rough seas or the Doldrums.

—**Ben Watson, Asheville**

John Hickman's poetry ranges widely over the vicissitudes of being and invites the reader's participation in the questions, desires, and delights of our lives. One poem includes the invitation to "tarry, look, listen, touch. grow, accept" and that is the essence of John's poetry and life. He does not mask the struggles with pain, loss and change or the big questions about God but is certain that Letting Go connects and enables us to discover fresh insight and clarity. I love these poems and the man who wrote them who is wise, down to earth, and willing to dream of what could be.

—**Dr. Elizabeth Canham,** *Ask the Animals*

Last Horizon

Last

4/10/21
For
Pat & George

John Bibb Hickman

John Bibb Hickman

Horizon

Selected Poems

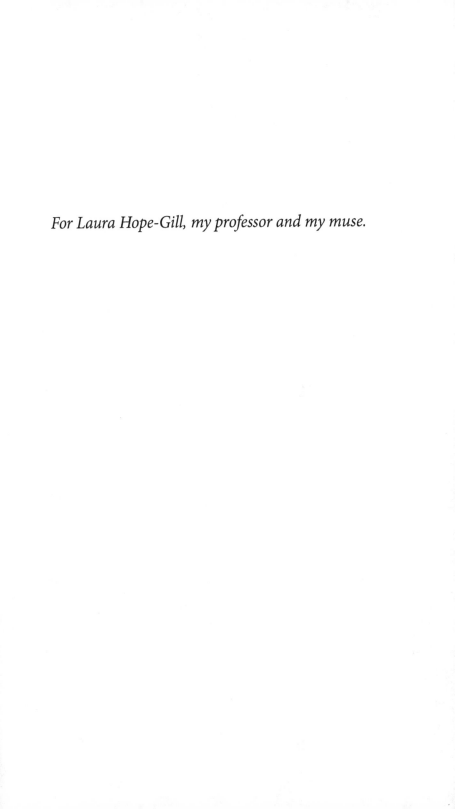

For Laura Hope-Gill, my professor and my muse.

Contents

A Sense of Place

A Sense of Spirit

A Sense of Intimacy

Be Careful!

Stay out of the road,
They'll run you over.
Stay out of the woods,
They'll eat you.

Stay off ladders,
You'll fall.
Stay out of the water,
You'll drown.

Stay out of the streets,
You'll get shot.
Stay out of crowds,
You'll get Corona Virus.

How many terrors must we face
Before we say, "Enough!"
And move on.

$C^h a_o S$

Emails unread and things I'll never use,
Jammed onto my shelves.
Papers spatter my desk like garbage
Tossed asunder in a gale.

Isn't it my job to put these items in order?

I select a single item,
Gaze upon it. Then, put it somewhere else,
Pushing chaos about, like a child avoiding
Nasty food on its dinner plate.

I take a document,
And stack it neatly on my desk
To pretend I'm cleaning house.
That's all I can do today.

ADHD? Dyslexia? Depression? Malaise?
Perhaps all of these and more.

But wait—I know!
Tomorrow's the day it will all come together,
As though by magic.

I shall simply wait until then.

Just like yesterday.

Bookshelves

Books inhabit my room: They taunt me.
Several demand to be opened now:
I nudge them, daily.

My mistress: That book I'm writing.
She begs me to go to bed with her and write.
She wants that, and only that.

I have a large book about poetry for healing:
Odes, exercises, advice.
Poetry does heal me.

Leonardo: I received him for Christmas.
Coated stock to enhance illustrations.
And how I love his dyslexic notebooks
Filled with lists and exciting ideas

Oh: Sister Fidelma, 7th century Irish sleuth,
Gaelic terms, Feudal norms, Irish vistas.
A fast read.

Mary Crow, Cherokee lawyer:
Spooky, Indian customs,
Taut plots.

Daily meditations for the writer:
Quotes. Interpretation. Advice.
A page for each day of the year.

My journal has a peacock on the cover
It sneers at me and
Commands all the books by my desk.

Beowulf and *Canterbury Tales* mock me from a
    nearby shelf.
Did you know Seamus Heaney translated
My copy of *Beowulf*?

Unsettled

It's that unsettled feeling
That something hasn't been done.
Or has been done wrong,
Or hasn't been done enough,
Or has been done too much,
Or something.

An unsettled feeling can sneak in, silently
Shoving its snout under your tent unawares.
But occasionally it will drop
Like a thunderbolt from Chicken Little's sky.
And your instinct tells you to ignore it
Because you believe
If you take the time to notice those inner thoughts,
A powerful creature will catch and eat you.

The Neanderthal hunter-gatherer
Rules your life from an unknown past.
And that six-year-old you know so intimately,
Decided decades ago, who you were.
And wants to run your life.

You think you should do something,
But that kid and the cave-dweller blind you.
Hiding your countless choices.

You hear them say something like,
"Pay no attention
To that person behind the curtain."

And that's what keeps you from noticing
That those drapes are nothing but an imaginary
        veil,
Hiding your beautiful face.

Eternal Stories

Their ages averaged nearly one hundred years.

All blessed with sharp minds and long memories.

When I left them that evening,

Still telling their stories,

I said to this trio of elders,

"God be with you till we meet again."

Did I really wish for God to join them?

Or was it Peace?

Or Serenity?

Or all of Creation?

I reveled in their cheer amid the pains of aging.

They leave stories.

Stories are eternal!

Goodnight Kiss

Matthew expected the time would come

When she would no longer recognize him.

One evening he kissed her good night:

She warned, "I don't think Matthew would like

  this."

He whispered, "Let it be our secret."

Though grieved by the loss, Matthew was pleased

That she still found him attractive.

Hollow Stares

Dementia's hollow stares haunt us.
Behind those eyes are souls
Hoping to engage the world
With bodies that no longer
Yield to engagement.
Or action.
Or desire.
Or perhaps even love.

We may attempt one-way conversation,
But dialog with empty space is difficult.
We know this, but it's hard to pass by
As though they didn't exist,
But just as hard to imagine them
As the vibrant people they once were.

We suffer with them.

Grief

I.
After all these years,
It can't end this way.
Our race to the finish
It can't be over so soon.

II.
My anger rises
With her,
With me and with them,
With God.

III.
My world is miserable.
Inhospitable.
What's the point
Of living this way?

IV.
That's it!
I'll try harder.
Then she'll return,
Won't she?

V.
Facing truth, I say,
We've had a wonderful ride!
I'm thankful for that.
Life continues.

Leaf Springs

Feelings dwell on
Leaf springs without shock absorbers.
But shocks aren't worth a damn when your ride
Lifts off the rails and soars out of control,
Leaving your emotions hanging
In midair knowing that
The landing could be a jolt
Of epic proportions.

Yearning

Amid noise, stench, scowls, loneliness,
I attend my lifelong love who is unaware
That this will be her home until she dies.
I yearn for her to seize the day
And make it hers again.

Knee Joint Replacement

Surgery done and
Pain is gone.
Fall colors will soon follow.

Let's Be Friends

Let's be friends, I and me.
We've known ourselves since infancy.
We've shared successes, shame and sorrows.
We have not many more tomorrows

So, make an effort: We might see
That I'm not so bad, nor is me.
We know that after all those years
We never truly shared our tears.

It's not about the good we've done
Though that might awe most anyone.
It's about ourselves, our character.
The sort of persons that we both are.

We are loved and loving human beings.
What is it that neither one was seeing?

Worthy
adjective: having worth or value

When you were but a child, you decided
that you were not worthy, though your
remarkable achievements shone brightly. Those
accomplishments were simply the things you did
naturally because you were talented.

You didn't know it, because nobody seemed to
take note, but those little feats of yours were truly
worthy. Those who were judging were looking for
blockbusters and you could offer nothing like that.

But look what you've done with your life! The
people you love and those who love you. Yes.
Without question, you are worthy. People follow
you because you are trust*worthy*. There's that word,
worthy.

Next time someone praises you, respond with
"Thank-you." Then, if you like, give credit to others
who helped, but then acknowledge your own
astonishing worth.

A Love Poem

He struggles to walk.
She watches with loving eyes.
As he staggers, then falls.
She encourages him.

He learns to walk.
She holds his immature body
Up to the sun
And chants, "Yess! Yess!"

He reaches a milestone.
She turns her head toward you and smiles
And with a thumb over her right shoulder
She says proudly, "That's my boy!"

What If You Had Never

What if you had never
Sailed upon the ocean,
What if you had never
Traveled far from home?

Then, how could you ever
Find another person
Who'd release your tether
And let your heart beat on?

What if you had never
Loved another deeply,
What if you had never
Opened up your soul?

Then, how could you ever
Find another person
Who'd release your tether
And let your heart beat on?

What if you had never
Tasted grief and sorrow,
What if you had never
Suffered all night long?

Then, how could you ever
Find another person
Who'd release your tether
And let your heart beat on?

But you have sailed upon the waters
And loved another deeply
And tasted grief and sorrow,
Your loving heart beats on.

Nearly There

Too busy to pause
Too focused to see
Too noisy to hear
Too sore to feel
Too old for youth
Too young to die

Tarry ...
Look ...
Listen ...
Touch ...
Grow ...
Accept ...

Please wait for me,
I'm barely hanging on,
But I think I'm almost there.

The Novel

Like the tar baby, it won't let me go.
I wrote long and hard to make it just so.
I thought I was finished, all words were in place.
It said not so fast boy, you see in this case,

You have lots more to do to make it just right.
Go ponder and scribble, write into the night,
For it will be with you from now to the end.
This story's not finished 'til more action is penned.

Reread every page, red pencil in hand,
Re-edit the story because it demands
Scenes with grand tension, action and sex,
With questions about what happens next.

It's not finished yet, while the book is still speaking
Do not despair, it just needs some tweaking!
And when you have finished, you will be so proud,
Of what you've accomplished you'll shout it out
        loud!

So, take heart about it,
You've got a good tale.
And soon you'll be happy
To see it for sale.

Haiku

I am "*now*."

Now can you see that

I'm gone now?

The Detroit News

One day, *The Beacon* appeared on my doorstep and brought with it an old memory because it smelled like the old *Detroit News*, which as a kid, I delivered to neighbors. In those days, a truck arrived shortly after school. The driver threw several neatly tied bundles of papers, toward the tiny, white hut on Bloomfield alley.

The hut smelled of these newspapers and of peanuts in a penny-dispenser. We boys munched peanuts while we folded our papers and tucked them so that we could throw them dead center onto subscriber's porches.

Oh, how I remember that freshly printed newspaper smell which is not the smell of the local paper today.

It is the dredged-up aroma of old memories.

In Honor of Thomas Wolfe

A stone, a leaf, an unfound door
These words haunt me, ever, ever more.
Stones don't move until they're thrown
A leaf is by the West-Wind blown.
A unfound door locks me in prison
Where I am trapped by my own decisions.

The Strange Estate

My copy arrived in the afternoon post
The Belfast poet's most recent publication,
Entitled: *The Strange Estate: New & Selected Poems.*

My issue was inscribed "Limited Edition"
And it was signed: *By the Poet*
In his own, Colicky, Gaeliky, sort of hand.

My copy is number fourteen of
Fifty-three limited copies.
Just what limits them, I do not know.
That's for St. Cecilia or perhaps St. Brigid
Or perhaps the other Brigid to say.

Though fifty-three is prime,
My "fourteen" is at best the sum of two primes.
But I do like my number.
It isn't a boastful NUMBER ONE,
Nor is it the bottom of the barrel.
Fourteen is a shy little number,
But I think its boldness will amuse you,
Hidden, as it is, in the middle of the pack!

But I cherish my book even more,
Knowing that my friend stayed up all night
Signing the title page so I'd be sure to have it
Before he returned with his family to Ireland.

I think I shall begin reading in the middle.

Perhaps on Page Fourteen.

A Sense of Place

Frosty Morn

He entered the wood on that frosty morn
To heal his heart where it was torn
By worries, pain, angst, and guilt
His heart's ache surged and then built

His sadness, was an awe-some stress
That his body said he must address
Or surely, he'd suffer some disease.
So on this path, he sought release.

He found a small secluded walk
And there, with tears, commenced to talk
To himself, and to his Creator,
About the ways that he might anchor

His mind and body to his soul
In a quest to make his whole life whole.
He saw so clearly in that place
There were no others in this race.

He thought of all the deeds he'd done
Had he injured anyone?
Or let his loved partner suffer?
Or failed in any way to offer

Love, compassion, and open ears
For stories from her hearts to hear?
And had he learned to love himself
Or left denial on the shelf?

He came home whole: He'd fought the fight,
Emerged with bliss, into the light
Freed at last to live his life
Amid struggles, doubt, and strife.

He was abruptly overcome
With peace and joy: he had won!
Ready to let new life begin,
He breathed in joy, exhaled his pain.

Where Am I From?

Where am I from?

After a joyful tryst,
They made love and kissed.
So because of this
Now I exist

Where am I from?

From love and a sigh.
I'm from far and nigh.
I am from the great blue sky.
And the mountains, high.

Where am I from?

I am from the fiery glow.
Of a world that seems so
Damaged that I don't know
Where next it can go.

Where am I from?

From people who
Thought they knew
What in the World to do.
And like me, had no clue.

So, where *am* I from?

When I leave this domain
You'll know my name.
And whence I came.
It'll be the same.

That's where I'm from.

Your World

I am your world, how do you behold me?
Am I your world of demons or your world of
      angels?
Am I your world of plenty, or are your desires
      elusive?

I have plenty for you, and nothing at all.
I am what I am, and you are all that I am,
For I am you. Nothing more.

I am your demons and I am your angels.
I hold your joy and hold your sorrows,
How you see me is your choice.

First Frost

Jake on the leash,
Following paths.
First frost covers
Lush autumn grass.

Sun behind us
Morning's shine
Each blade sparkles
As a diamond.

Fourth Thursday in November

Walking in the crisp, cold air,
Snowflakes fall about us.

Odors escape from houses,
First, aromas of cooking turkeys.
Then the smell of wood-smoke.

Quiet. Quiet.
Almost
The
Quiet
Of a
Heavy
Snow-
fall.

No dogs appear.
Not even Bluto, who often
Announces our passing.

The snowflakes continue to fall.
Not enough for white.
But enough.

Returning home,
The roast is ready.
We give thanks.

Hopetown Light

This light is a wonderful sight!
Built on its site
In Hopetown Harbour
One hundred sixty years ago

Tall, with red and white bands
And topped by a light
So that mariners might
Never ground on the bight.

A staircase spirals into the top
Of the old stone cone
Where the light and its lens
Float on a circular mercury pan.

Like a grandfather's clock
A brass weight pulled to the top
By the keeper of the light
Every two hours through the night.

The weight drops down
And a bell wakes the keeper
Whose sound sleep is broken
So, he goes around

To see that the light is still lit,
Then cranks the weight 'till it
Reaches the top and sits.
Turning the light as it drops down the pit.

A gauze sock is pumped
With pressurized lamp oil
Then the sock is lit
Like a Coleman lantern.

The flame shines far through a
Fresnel lens so the mariner
When the fog is dense
Can see farther.

Surely engineers
Could have designed this thing
To last all night
Then the bell ring.

But wait! Let me think…
A ship takes two hours
From first sight of the light
Before crashing the shores of the bight.

So the engineers cleverly designed
It to wake up the keeper
To get out of his sleep where
He'd check on the light
To make sure that it's bright.

Tree Frogs

Caribbean breezes
Moon and stars above
Little tree frogs chirp
!ng !ng !ng.

Little Harbour

A member of the Cruising Club of America invited me to join their annual Bahamas cruise. We anchored in Little Harbour on Great Abaco Island where the residents, for an exorbitant fee offered to prepare us a pig roast. Since the place was little more than a wilderness, with little else to do, we accepted and had a wonderful feast. Here's a reflection:

Pit fires blazed upon the beach
Like buccaneers of old
In this cove, were pirates too,
Modern. But just as bold.

They spied our happy little fleet
Two dozen cruisers all
With spars and ropes and billowed sails.
And masts so very tall.

Pirate Pete was on the shore
He runs the Harbour Bar
Serving sailors from the sea
Who'd come there from afar.

The Cruising Club was on a tour
Sailing in the Bahamas
Among the sailors were some daddies
Others, they were mamas.

A blazing fire upon the beach
They fired up at dawn
To roast a brace of wildest boars
For us to feed upon.

I call them Pirates, that's because
These cheerful Island folk
Charged us all the highest price
For charred pig meat and smoke.

We joined the pirates roasting boars
With wine and rum and beer
All the trimmings they set out
Filled us all with cheer.

When the party finally quit,
The tide by then ran out
Leaving many boats aground
But ours just bobbed about.

Landlubbers hear this lesson dear
When anchored for the night,
Beware the natives and their rum,
Who rob without a fight.

Kindergarten

What, kindergarten taught me:

I learned that miss Mary had a skunk fur coat, but it didn't smell.
I learned that naps were boring, and you had to pretend you were asleep.
I learned that your mom would scold you when you got paint on your clothes.
I learned that some kids were nice; others were bullies.
I learned that you shouldn't play with matches. (I lit a pile of leaves on the playground and another kid tattled.)
I learned that the cloak room always smelled of bologna sandwiches.
I learned that Alice was mean to everyone, not just me.
I learned that you could learn the alphabet just by singing a song.
I learned that there were kids that didn't look much like me.
I learned that you had to share stuff.
I learned that reading was fun, but better when there were pictures in the book.
I learned that girls don't have wee-wees. They have vertical smiles where theirs ought to be.

I learned that your older brother would pretend he
didn't know you, even when you said, "Hi!"
I learned that you had to stand in line sometimes,
and you got angry when other kids took cuts.
I learned that your mom wasn't always there to
save you.
I learned to lookout for my friends.
I learned that I had a lot to learn.

Hungarian National Museum
Budapest

First, the Romans, then Mongol Tartars,
The Magyars, the Turks, The Austrians,
The Nazis, and The Soviets.
Hungary rarely ruled herself,

So, she has neither political
Nor military heroes of her own,
And her kings were largely unsung.

The Hungarian National Museum displays
Scant pictures of generals or politicians.
The people don't celebrate them because
They are not the people's heroes.

Instead, the museum features paintings
Of ordinary people living ordinary lives:
Hungarians celebrating life!

Drunken peasants laughing
In a dusty, messy, earthy, rustic tavern.
Very unlike the neat drinking scenes
Of the Old Dutch Masters.

A couple having a serious discussion
She might be telling her boyfriend,
"Mattias, I think I'm pregnant."

A young girl is shown
Gathering sheaves
In a field by an
Oxcart which is mired in mud.

Posed saints wearing preposterous cassocks and
    jewelry,
Stand among Byzantine icons
And paintings of the Ural Mountains.

And in the museum's entrance hall,
A large, bronze bulldog
Greets visitors, while it
Bites fleas off its butt.

Leaves

Autumn leaves, peach-pink
With tinges of tan,
hang on, retaining the last gasp
of summer's bounty.

We listen to the rain that shares the very water
that nurtured those leaves last spring and summer,
and will soon wash them away to make room
for next year's new, green, crop.

These leaves, in their annual cycle
are metaphors for our lives as
we are born and then
reborn every season.

And Then You Vanished

Across the street,
Nearly hidden by slender trees
Bearing autumn leaves that flutter in the breeze.
There is a brick house
With a solid-green awning over the walk.

I imagine that you are sitting by the paned window
Above the awning and also see these trees.
And I also suppose that you ponder the leaves with
        me
So in my mind, we connect, if only for this instant.

Wind swirls down the street striping the leaves
And your image disappears from the window.
I had hoped to reconnect
But as with the leaves, you vanished.

Ledbury

I spent the night in an ancient hotel
In the Herefordshire village of Ledbury.
Every window lined with thrift and petunias
Also above the door of the library.

An Anglican church as old as the inn
Anchored its graceful square.
With a pub so old that I imagined that
Chaucer might have tarried there.

Many years later, I discovered
It was John Masefield's birthplace
Who invites me to enjoy a merry yarn
And a dream from a tome in my bookcase.

He gives me a tall ship
And stars to steer her by.

Bookstore Cruise

The cruise offered many wonders
There were cliffs and fjords and coves,
And organized shore excursions
To visit famous sites adored by tourists.

But when he ventured ashore,
He organized his own outings.
A pathway along a rocky shore
Or through some woods or into a quaint village.

In every town, he found a bookstore.
And in each, asked the clerk,
Who is your favorite local author,
And which of theirs is your favorite book?

Oh, that would be Mr. Coffin.
He's a hermit, you know. Lives in a crude hut
On the shingles under the dunes.
Occasionally stops in
To see if any of his books have sold.
Some always have.

Miss LeClair lives in Minnesota,
But she's here every summer on her boat.
Look. We all love this one of hers,
It's a murder mystery.
Takes place right here.
Could have happened, too.

Sit over there if you wish.
Here's a cup of tea.
Read the novel.
If you like it, we'll wrap it for you.

So you do want the book, then.
Thanks. Here's your change.
If you like, you may drop it in this jar
For our historic preservation fund.

Cheers. I hope you enjoy her book.
It's part of a series.
Write us when you are ready.
We'll ship you a sequel

Goodbye. Where
Did you say you were from?
Oh. We hope you will return some day.
Have a wonderful cruise!

Lunch at the Red Barn

I ordered lunch at a little red barn
That had free coffee and conversation.
They had bait and crawlers too
In the cooler next to the cheeses.

Neighbors sat to greet and chat
I sat at another table In my knit hat.
I couldn't read the menu high on the wall
So, I asked her to make me her favorite.

Her favorite was, she said:
Grilled cheese and bacon on wheat,
With tasty fries on the side.
She's sixteen and fixed the sandwich.

I took this back with me
To the Center where I shared
My lunch with Sister Mary Paul
And my dear daughter.

We laughed about the bait.

My Stuff

All this stuff.
Items of financial value.
Spiritual treasures.
Cherished memories.
Instruments:
    Harp, Whistle, & Box.
Electronics.
Car. Home. Friends. Family. Children.

This isn't really my stuff
It's all on loan.
I must return it all
On the last day.

I shall keep nothing except
My wedding ring:

I will take that with me.

TERMINAL Ⓔ

They swelter elbow-to-elbow, awaiting delayed
flights in the fusty departure hall.
Children whimper, teens titter, people pace with
scant notion of where they truly wish to go,
and meander among the gates like cattle in a
corral.

Loud announcements shatter the dank, stale air:
"we will now begin… "do not accept…
"smoking only… "keep your… "do not allow
unknown persons… But aren't we all unknown
persons?

Each of us intends to return home or meet
associates or seek adventure—perhaps a tryst. The
great hall will clear by day's end when domestics
enter to discard the detritus of the long day.

Most, if not all passengers will reach their intended
destinations if not their destinies. Most, if not all
will fulfill their plans if not their desires.

Voluptuous

He senses the grained texture of this rocky ledge
and surveys the freemasonry of the foliage
beneath. For him, this place is far more sacred
than the red bricks or sculpted granite of an urban
cathedral.

A womb of voluptuous mountains enfolds the
ancient forest. Noonday sun pierces a dark
trail below the overstory, projecting cheerful
punctuations onto the ground.

As he listens, the leaves chatter among themselves.
He chews the sweet stem of a ribwort while
eucalyptus, pine, and skunkweed create heady
aromas.

Crickets converse as bird songs fill the air and a
snake with black velvet scales slithers from clump
to clump, tasting the air with its forked, crimson
tongue.

Immersed in the valley's texture, tastes, sounds,
odors, colors, he finds tranquility here.
As nowhere else on earth.

A Sense of Spirit

Holy Ground

The valley nestles far below,
Seed pods float like falling snow.
The air refreshed, by recent rain
Renews the forest once again.

> *Hush—my children.*
> *Can't you see?*
> *This is Holy Ground.*

Whistling wind excites the day
Pampas grass, like new mown hay,
Wafts perfume while crickets speak.
Tears of joy drain down my cheek.

> *Hush—my children*
> *Can't you see?*
> *This is Holy Ground.*

A bird above sings ancient songs
A deer appears and then is gone
In the stream with water fresh,
A trout jumps up and makes a splash

> *Hush—my children*
> *Can't you see?*
> *This is Holy Ground.*

Silken grasses, rustling leaves
Orchestrate a world that breathes.
Sapphire sky with Earth below
Complete this valley's grand tableau.

Speak—my children,
For now you see that
This is Holy Ground.

Anthropos

A long time ago,
(By your reckoning anyhow)
I set the Universe in motion
And watched to see what would happen.
    You should have been there to see it!

It was my final attempt to create one that could
        sustain itself.
I fiddled with gravitational constants, light speeds,
And myriad other factors to get it just right.

First there was only the detritus of failed universes.
Then, I saw a great flash! I think it was green.
Could have been orange.
Can't remember; been too long.
    For a while, there was nothing but gas,

Then, slowly.
Ever so slowly,
(By your reckoning anyhow)
    Stars appeared.

I gazed in awe at their splendor.
None of my other universes
Was anything like this one!

The gases condensed into more stars.
Millions of them. Billions. Millions of billions!
Some white, some red, some blue.
    Some were just black holes!

One star exploded.
Then another. And another.
And while they were exploding,
    Newer stars formed

Then, slowly.
Ever so slowly,
(By your reckoning anyhow)
    The swirling chaos created planets to orbit those stars.

A few stars, twins, spun around each other.
One planet orbited in a figure eight around a pair
    of stars,
I think she did it simply to amuse me.

Then, slowly.
Ever so slowly,
(By your reckoning anyhow)
    Your Sun and Earth appeared in the middle of a
        galaxy!

Formed from stardust.
Blue and white and green.
And HOT!

Other planets appeared, too.
The big one you call Jupiter was so large
That its gravity shielded your planet from
Cosmic bombardment
Which would have prevented life on Earth.

Then, slowly.
Ever so slowly,
(By your reckoning anyhow)
   Creatures appeared on your planet:
   Amoebas, worms, fish, birds, mammals.
   Even I couldn't imagine such a vast variety.

Your species differed from the others,
For you could anticipate your own death.
Though ancient scribes wrote that death was a
      curse,
You learned that it wasn't that at all,
But was a necessary fact of life.
And with that knowledge, you learned
   To make the best of your brief time here.

Then, slowly.
Ever so slowly,
(By your reckoning anyhow)
    You learned to respect your Earth.
    To enjoy its beauty and gather its bounty.

One fateful day, one of your scribes wrote
That he thought you should subdue your Earth.

It was on that day that you learned avarice,
And became addicted to greed.
And went to war with each other
    To sustain your gluttony.

You subdued it all right!
Noxious compounds increased your harvests,
But killed fragile creatures.

You overfished the seas with machinery,
And filled your forests and oceans
    With trash.

Industrial pollution changed your climate faster
    than
Natural forces could adapt.
And warmer temperatures helped pathogens
    spread,
    Threatening your entire species.

This was all your doing.
You subdued it until there was nothing left to kill.
    Then your planet died with you.

Do you remember?

Sudden Life

Without warning, the large truck halted in our
lane. Our driver noticed too late, and we collided
with the stopped vehicle at highway speed.
It is said that pilots and others, when faced with
imminent doom, emit epithets.
Curiously, I didn't do that: My only thought was:
This is it: I'm finished.

Then a brackish taste entered my mouth: Air-bag
powder... *Still alive!*

But for the airbag, I would have died. Would have
been so easy, too. Takes no effort at all.

Dying is easy. Living—that's what's hard.
Understanding that death will surely come makes
living choices more thoughtful. Yet I'm not ready
to go now.

Still got stuff to do.

Mortal Beings

There is no cure for birth and death save to enjoy the interval. The dark background which death supplies brings out the tender colors of life in all their purity.
– GEORGE SANTAYANA

I hear the blackbird sing its song,
He sleeps with open eye.
He doesn't have the leastest thought
That someday he may die.

Is it blessing or a curse?
It's neither one to him.
As for me, I think it worse,
To never know my end.

Now please don't get me wrong on this
I shall not hasten Death.
But knowing life will someday end
Gives meaning to my breath.

If I were blackbird in my prime,
I'd never dream of dying.
And never know my song so sweet
Would stop in midst of trying.

So, Death I celebrate with you
I know that I am mortal.
I must get my Earth's work done
Before I reach your portal.

Universal Questions

Is ours a deist universe
Wound and set by a Creator,
To unwind eternally
And adjust to eco changes?

Or is it anthropic, having an
Intelligent Creator establishing everything
Micromanaging it in real time
To guarantee emergence of human life?

Or is it something else altogether?

And whoever lit that big explosion?
And how was that instant chosen?
Such are Universal Questions...

Sonnet on Kundera and Gödel

Milan Kundera said: "Questions with no answers set the limits of human possibilities and desxcribe the boundaries of human existence." The twentieth century mathematician, Kurt Gödel showed that mathematical statements exist which have no answers. If this is so, even in the highly structured world of mathematics, how much more does it apply to the messy business of living?

We'd like to believe that we live an unbounded life.
However, Gödel and Kundera stop us short.
They say that we are limited by
Fundamental, unanswerable questions.

They say we cannot fly into an unknown world.
Only science fiction can take us there.
They say we are Earthbound:
Unable to soar with the eagle

But we also know that, if we do reach for the stars,
We shall not get nematodes under our fingernails.
The Universe is within our grasp for we consist of
    Stardust.
So, get behind us Gödel. Away Kundera.
We are one with the universe.
So there!

Epiphany

It has been so long
I can't remember why we took that journey,
Or why we packed so much treasure,
Or why we travelled at night,
On the frigid Naphtali desert,

Or why we crested the mountain,
Or why we entered Bethlehem,
Or why we stopped at that dusty inn.

I can remember that it was cold,
I remember that the trip had been long.
I remember our minions complaining of sore feet.
I remember my two companions
Wished to pause for the night.

I also remember the crowds in Bethlehem.
I remember that the inn asked exorbitant prices,
But we secured a room because we could pay.

I remember the kindly innkeeper
Who put up a man and his pregnant wife
In the stable where the animals
Would keep them warm.

For some reason, we visited the stable.
There, we saw a newborn boy.
For some reason, we thought it was special.
For some reason, we shared our bounty—
Myrrh, frankincense, gold.

Luke said we followed a star.
Yes, but it wasn't a special star—
We followed the sun by day
And the stars by night.

Luke said we were wise men.
No, we were very wealthy
But we were not wizards.

Luke said we were warned in a dream,
To leave by a different route.
No, we simply travelled over the next mountain
To continue our journey.

Luke said what we saw in the stable
Was a miracle.

That was so.
But isn't every birth a miracle?

For Centuries Uncounted

For centuries uncounted,
We've looked for the nature of god,
With firm faith in books having
Notions some think are odd.

For centuries uncounted,
We've claimed god to be
A Substance. A person.
A Him. And a She.

For centuries uncounted,
We've struggled to show
That we alone, are the
Ones in the know.

For centuries uncounted,
We've sought god in church
And finding few answers,
We continue our search.

And since the Creator
Is unknowable, infinite, ineffable
God shall for uncounted centuries
Remain incomprehensible.

It Was Friday.

With scant to do on our Sabbath,
We welcomed the excitement of a crucifixion.
We went there to watch others,
(Thankfully not us), tortured to death.

This may seem bizarre,
But do you remember the lynchings
You conducted against your own people?
Your victims were far more innocent than
Some souls we murdered at Calvary that day.

The doomed carried heavy crosses.
Unlike your fancy Christian symbols, they were
        crude tees
One of the prisoners, a man they called Jesus,
Wearily trudged his way up the hill.
Some him helped carry his heavy oaken cross,
Not out of compassion, but to hasten the spectacle.

Roman custom offered a concession to the Jews:
They let us choose a prisoner to free.
The one we knew best was Barabbas.
Of course we chose him.
You see, on that day Jesus was just a minor
        criminal.
Didn't even make the short-list.

A noisy crowd gathered.
Some sat on grey and white striped blankets.
The wealthy raised tents to shield them
From the noon-day sun.

Vendors appeared with enormous straw baskets
Filled with loaves, and figs, and grapes and olives.
There was joking, feasting, music, and merriment.
Children laughed and played hide and seek
     amongst the gathering throng.

The Romans forced the prisoners onto crosses
Drove stakes into their hands and their feet.
And raised them upright to hang and to die.
I was near the man they called Jesus.
Some said he spoke to his god.
I heard nothing.
You see, the crucified die of asphyxiation.
They cannot speak.
I believe your negroes had it right:
"He didn't say a mumblin' word."

After the prisoners were dead and broken,
And with no further amusement,
The crowd dispersed.

Afraid that they might be next,
Jesus's disciples ran… hid.
Only the women remained with the body.

Answers

He loves the questions
And statistical analysis,
Because it permits him
To praise mystery and doubt,
And to bracket God's mind,
Imagining where answers might lurk.

He knows with certainty
He will never know precisely
What the answers are, exactly,
Except within the limits
Of statistical ambiguity.

He never trades good questions
For mere answers.

Beyond

Beyond the merchants,
Beyond bells clanging above red alms pots,
Beyond vendors' booths and raucous pseudo-
      music,
Invading shopping malls.

Beyond world news reports,
Beyond the excitement of children, young and old,
Beyond the solstice, and believers, and the pious,
Beyond kneeling sinners,
Beyond the Earthly.

For the blessed few,
Christmas creates a time
Of tranquility and reflection,

A time for stories…
Family stories,
Biblical stories and myths,
Reflective stories,
Stories: The core, of our being.

Our world pauses its awful spiral,
If only for a moment,
And lets us renew our souls.

Board of Directors

After the sham trial, we watched
As they murdered him in the cruelest way.
He did not die from the spear
Thrust into his side by the cowardly centurion,
Who attacked a victim already nailed down,
And who could neither fight nor flee.
No.
He died from asphyxiation, on a crude cross.

Several men calling themselves disciples followed
          him.
They were his board of directors.
And having witnessed his murder,
They fled fearing that they might be next.
One never knows in a totalitarian world.

It was the women who stayed.
They wrapped him in linen
And secured the shallow rock tomb that
Lazarus had prepared for himself.
They laid him for his final rest.
And wedged, a large, rock
Over the tomb, to seal it.

The following day, although the men had fled,
The women were back.
Mary thought she recognized her friend, arisen.
And she told the world so.

Once the men heard that it was safe,
They reappeared and took over.
"Man's work."
Women can't handle this, they said.
And so it's been for over two millennia.

Even today, churches, schools
And the Vatican say
"No women need apply"
After all, were there any men on *his*
Board of directors?

Of course not.
Why start now?

Cosmos

a rare
fleeting
event
is all it takes
to realize there is something
beyond your touch
beyond your understanding
beyond your imagination

that
singular
instant
connects
your
soul
neither to the Earth
nor to the Moon
nor to the Sun
nor to the Stars

but for just an instant—

to the Cosmos.

Creator

Jesus said,
"No one comes to the Father,
Except through me."

Joseph Campbell asks,
"Then how about to the Mother?"

You may ask,
"Then, what about to the Creator?"

If there is a Father, would he not come
To all his beloved children?

If there is a Mother,
Would she not do the same?

If there is a Creator,
As surely there must be,
The Wonder of Creation
Comes to all of us in its fullest Glory,
All by Itself.

Inheritance

Somewhere between "I never knew my father" and
W. S. Gilbert's Poo-Bah, who claimed
He could trace his ancestry to a
"Primordial Blob of Protoplasm,"
We struggle to discover our ancestry.
And businesses thrive by offering answers:
Just send them your DNA.

So, why should we care?
What difference does it make whether
Your great-great-great was a king, a politician,
Or highwayman?
If you knew for certain that Midas or,
Aristotle, or Job was your ancestor,
Would it change your life in the least?

But we do share a fascination about
People whose traditions have been
Passed to us through thousands of years,
Just as we wonder at birds whose
Migration routes follow prehistoric riverbeds
That disappeared long before we were here to see.

We ponder questions like:
How did our language evolve, and where?
Through how many generations have
My blue eyes passed, or my father's red hair
Or the "Bibb Foot," a trait our mother said
My brother and I inherited.

We care about inherited mysteries the way
We care about the Creation story.
We want to know how and when and where it all
        happened.
When we learn that, will we not discover…
Why we're here?

Letting Go

As we mature, a time comes
When we accept the notion
That for us, many things
Will never get better.

And we acknowledge that
Next year may be worse
Perhaps next month
Maybe tomorrow.

"Just wait until next year"
No longer helps,
For now we know there are dreams
We must abandon.

Letting go is a learned art
One we never considered
When we acquired all
That we now cherish

So how do we learn to let go
And find the grace
To look back upon
Our unique, astonishing life?

Be thankful,
And find the courage to say,

Amen.

Lights Out

Like Muslim funeral ablutions,
I washed my body
The night before with Dexedrine
And the following morning, too.

They set me on a gurney
And inserted an intra-venous needle
Into my right hand and wrapped me
With meticulous care.

They took me to a solitary solemn site
Where I stayed for a spell.
Then they injected something
Into the needle, Silently, serenely...

Lights out!

I was no longer aware of this life...

Is that how my death will be?
Here one moment and gone
In the very next instant...
Silently,
Serenely,
Forever?

Or will it be a passage like a plane ride:
Fasten your belts.
Takeoff.
Fly.
Land later on the other side.

I expect it will just be lights out.

Razor's Edge

That precarious moment between
The No-Where and The Here.
Like death, dancing on a razor's edge.
What is the No-Where? Where is The Here?

And what on Earth is the purpose of it all?
Why does it matter how we address a dying
      woman?
Or a coo to a baby emerging from the womb?
It is never just about them, is it?

Music

It's such a miracle that ancient music speaks over the centuries through written scores. We hear Bach's Fugues, or Palestrina's chants as clearly as though these composers lived with us today. We marvel how twelve tones and seven Grecian modes can generate so many different moods. Notes, rhythm, and mode can yield a plethora of tunes: Celtic, German, English, Arab and many, many, more. The English language needs twenty-six letters and several punctuation marks to write a sonnet, but musicians can compose one using but twelve notes and seven modes.

Sacred Candles

In solemn lines, grateful or grieving or broken
people approach little baskets of candles and each
selects one or two. They proffer their little tapers to
receive a passing of flames and once lit, supplicants
quietly plant theirs in a sandbox.
Afterward, everyone feels a great outpouring of
love arising from the plethora of tiny blazes.

Nuptials

Sisters, brothers, aunts, uncles, cousins, and estranged spouses: Lay down your spears for just a moment, and join each other in wishing the boy and the girl long life and happiness in the desperate hope that this time—just this once—the couple will live happily ever after.

Susan

Hello Susan, it's me…
Mom.

I didn't know how else to reach you,
So here's my note…
I'll leave it here in this little chapel.

Sleep well, my beautiful child.
Know that I love you

Always and Forever

Mom

The Loss of a Child

how do you face the loss of a child
born alive too weak to live
but just a few days in an incubator

how do you face the loss of a child
eagerly anticipated from the first twinkle
to the erotic act of conception
to preparing for its arrival
to months of anticipation

how do you face the loss of a child
when you are young and vulnerable
and are just beginning to know your partner
and haven't yet begun to know yourself

how do you face the loss of a child
before you have dealt with the world's realities
its indifference to who you are
or whence you came

how do you face the loss of a child
when you imagine the joy of letting
it show you your world
and decades later wondering
what sort of person it might have become

how do you ever face the loss of that child

Last Horizon

Were my home upon the sea,
With a boat, a sail, the ocean and me,
Toward every compass point, I'd sail,
And reef the main before each gale.

At one with porpoises and with the birds,
In a place for which I'd have no words
To describe the simple ecstasy
Of sailing where the wind blows free.

And when I tire of every port,
I'd haul my anchor and depart,
To sail before a flood tide rising,
Reaching for my last horizon.

There to drop my final anchor
And give thanks to my Creator

Acknowledgements

I wish to thank Professor Laura Hope-Gill, my muse and mentor, for extracting the poet from within me and helping to assemble this collection of poems. I wish also to thank the *Live Poets Society* of Deerfield Episcopal Retirement Community for patiently listening as I recited several of these poems and for encouraging me to continue writing them.

I am indebted to AD Tinkham who graciously granted permission to copy his painting, *Rough Day* for the cover of this book.

CPSIA information can be obtained
at www.ICGtesting.com
Printed in the USA
FSHW012331270321
79912FS